Stunning Pictures of Sunsets And Sky's For The Modern Day Genius

By Sir Richard Sullivan The 3rd

ISBN: 10:153287572X
ISBN-13: 978-1532875724

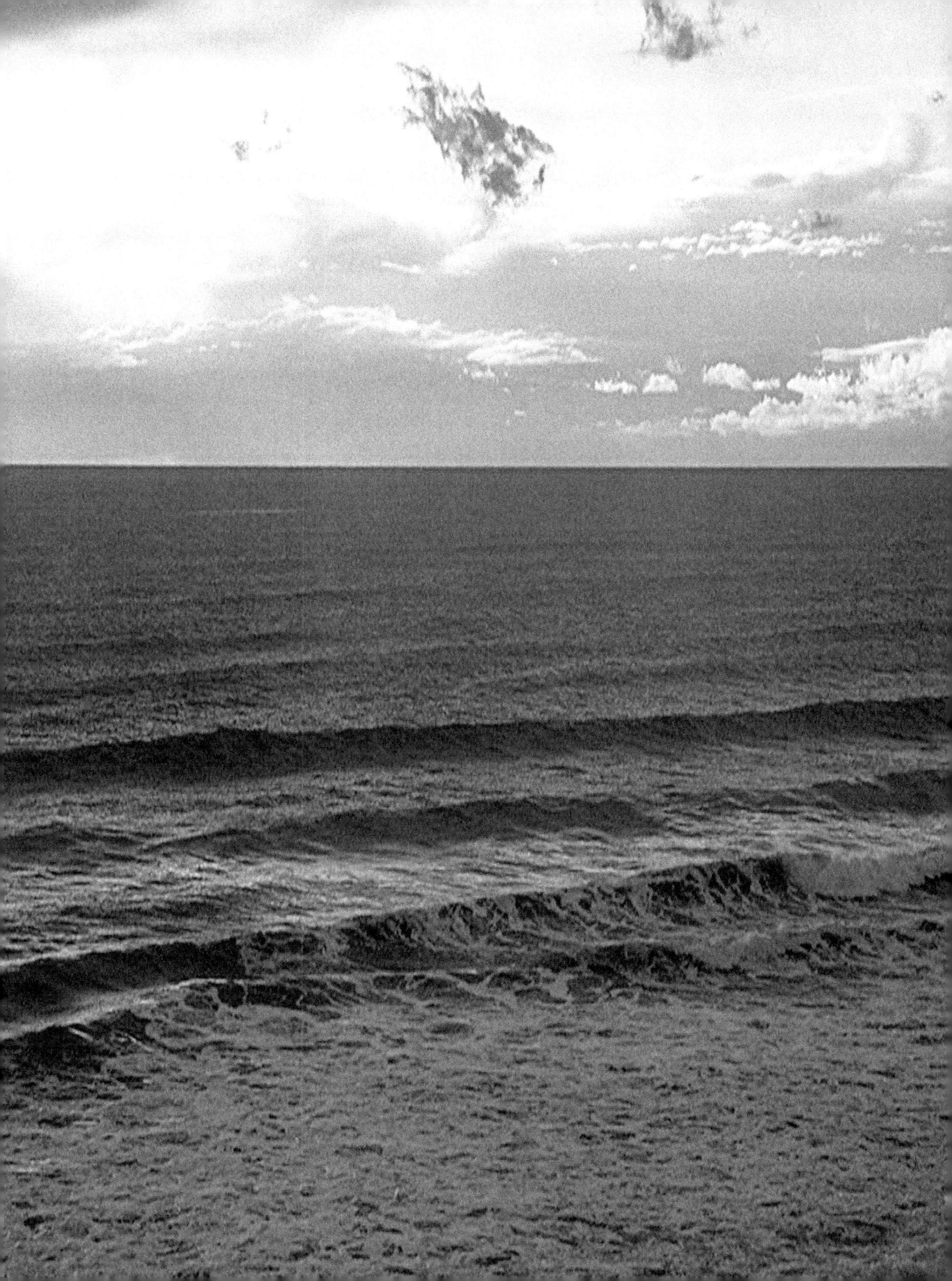

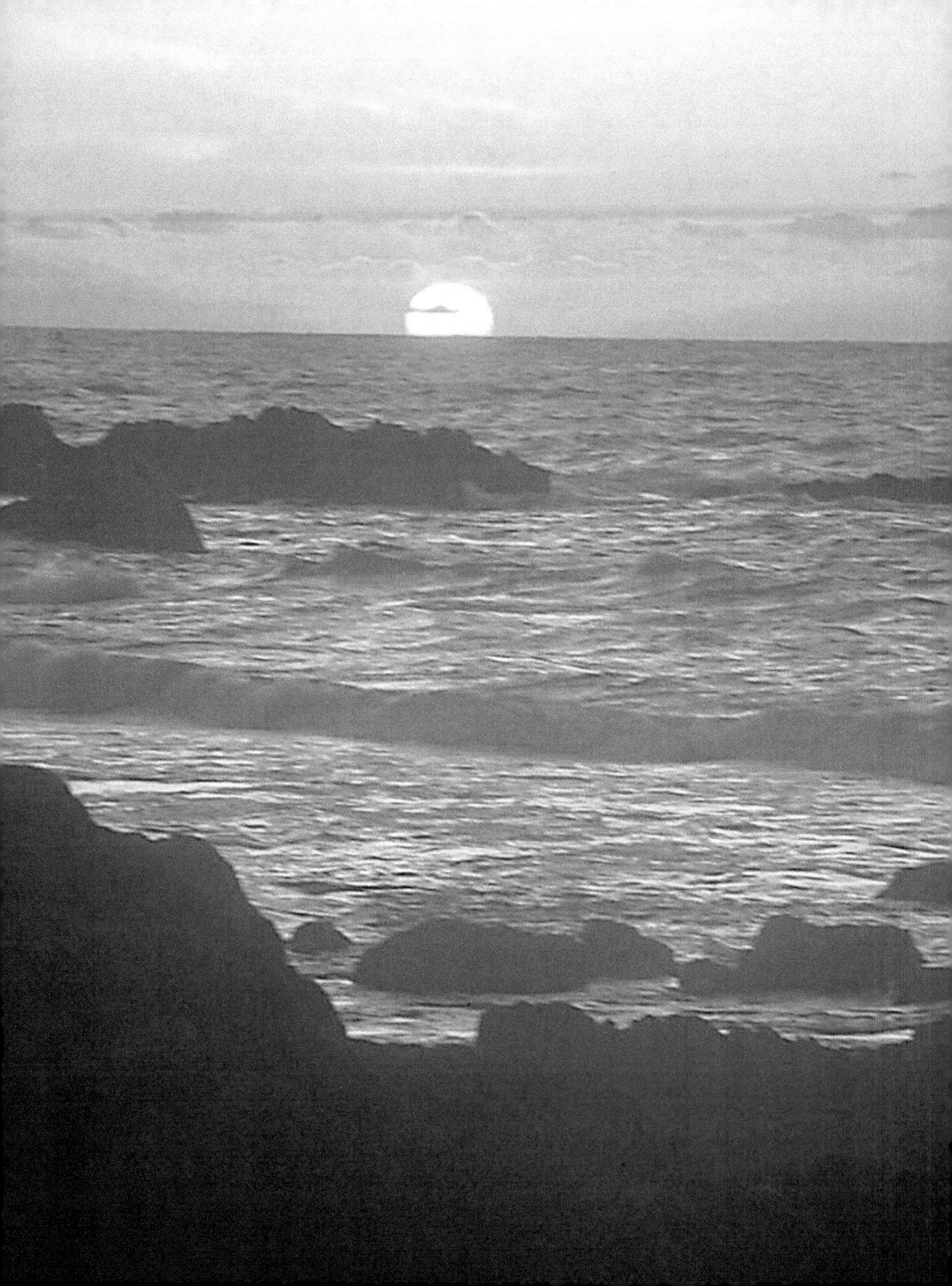

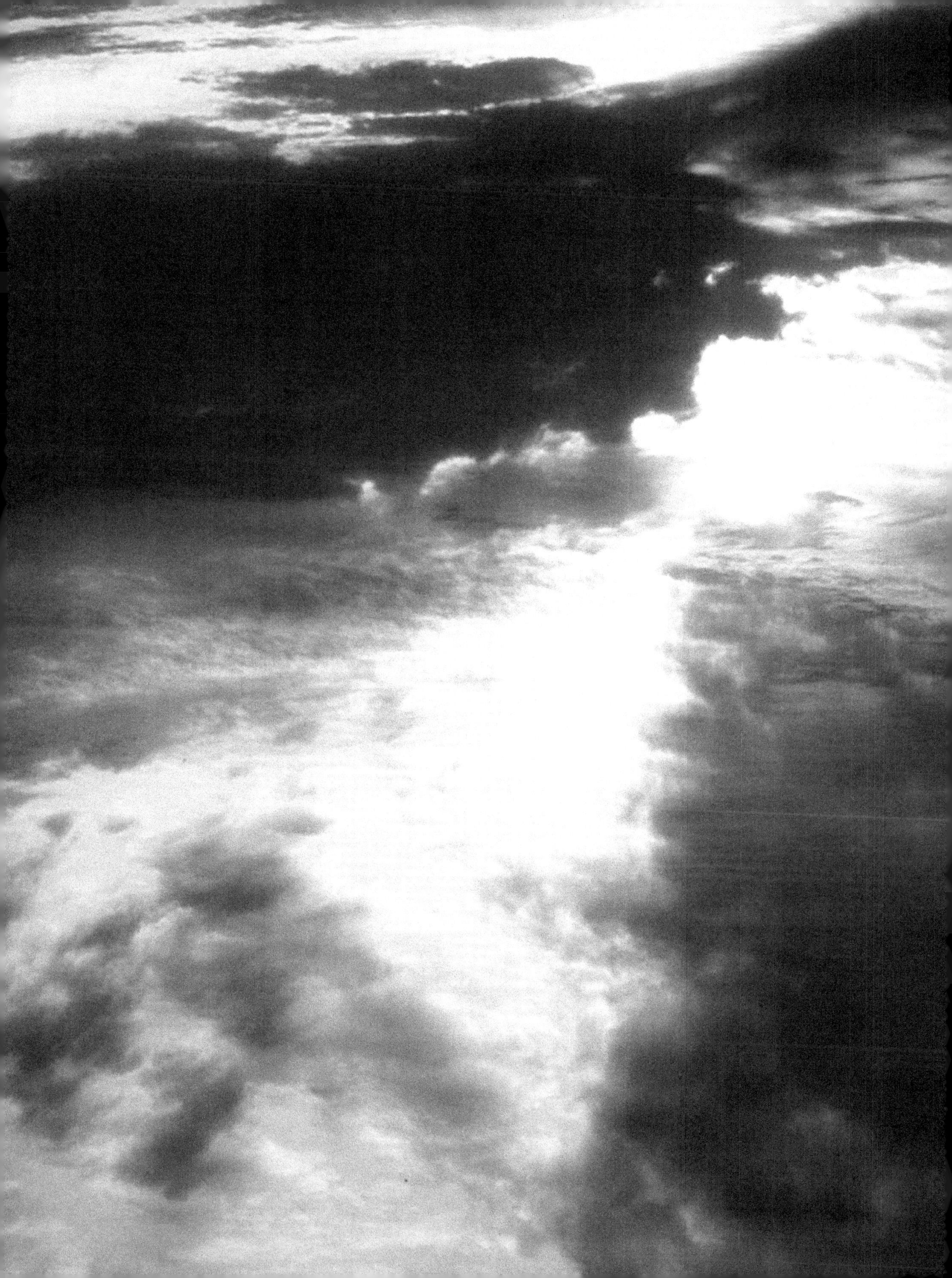

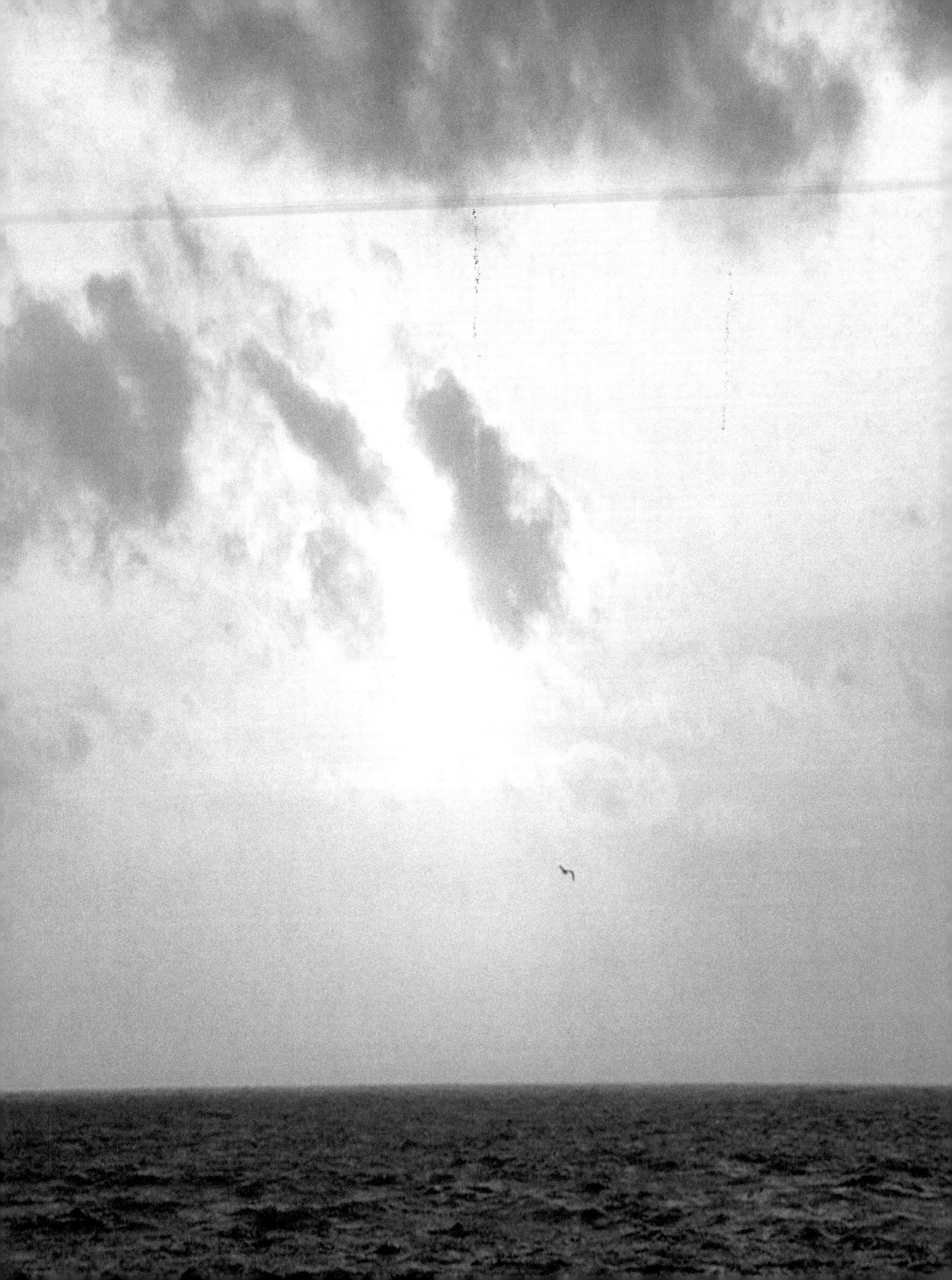

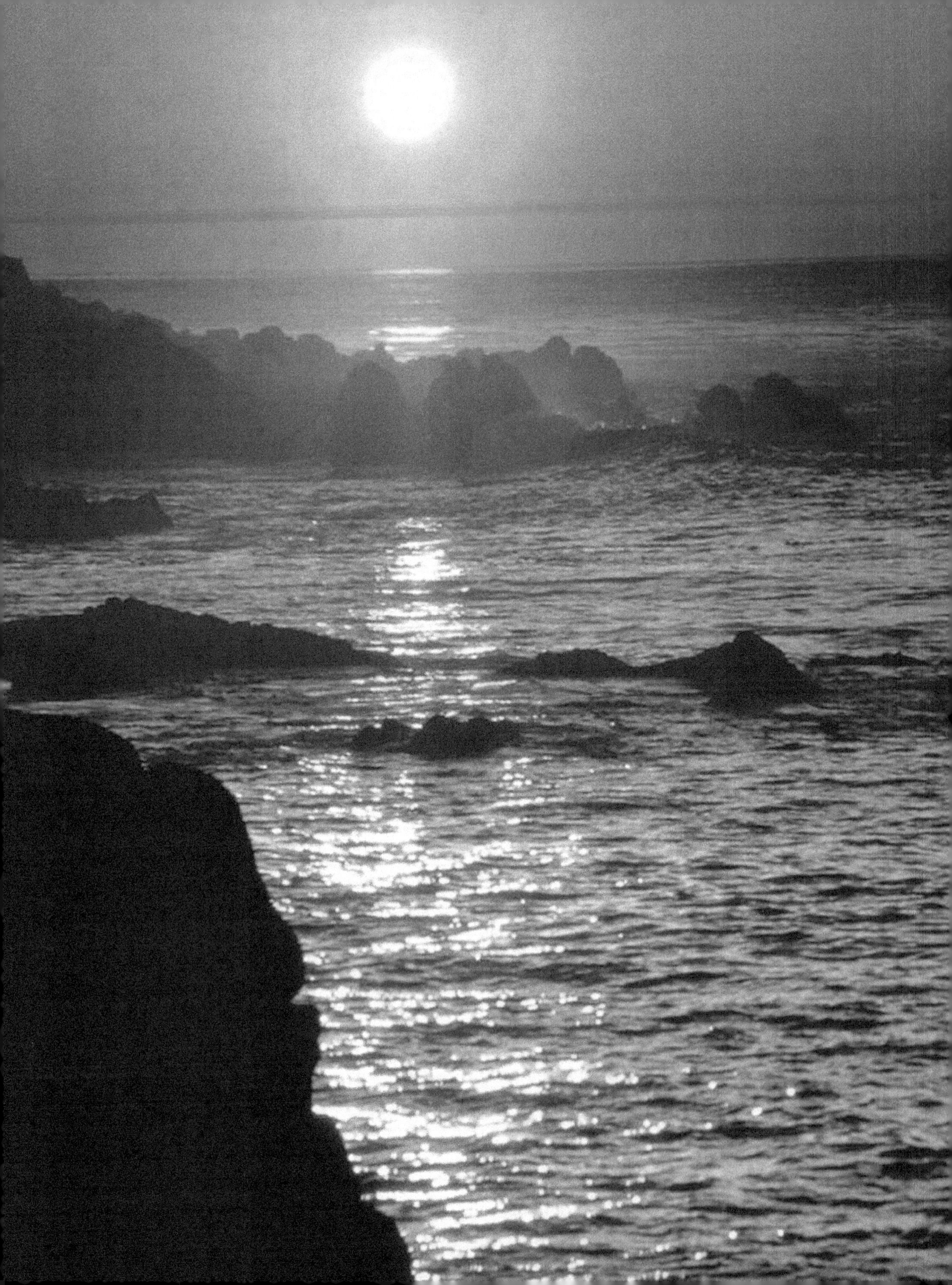

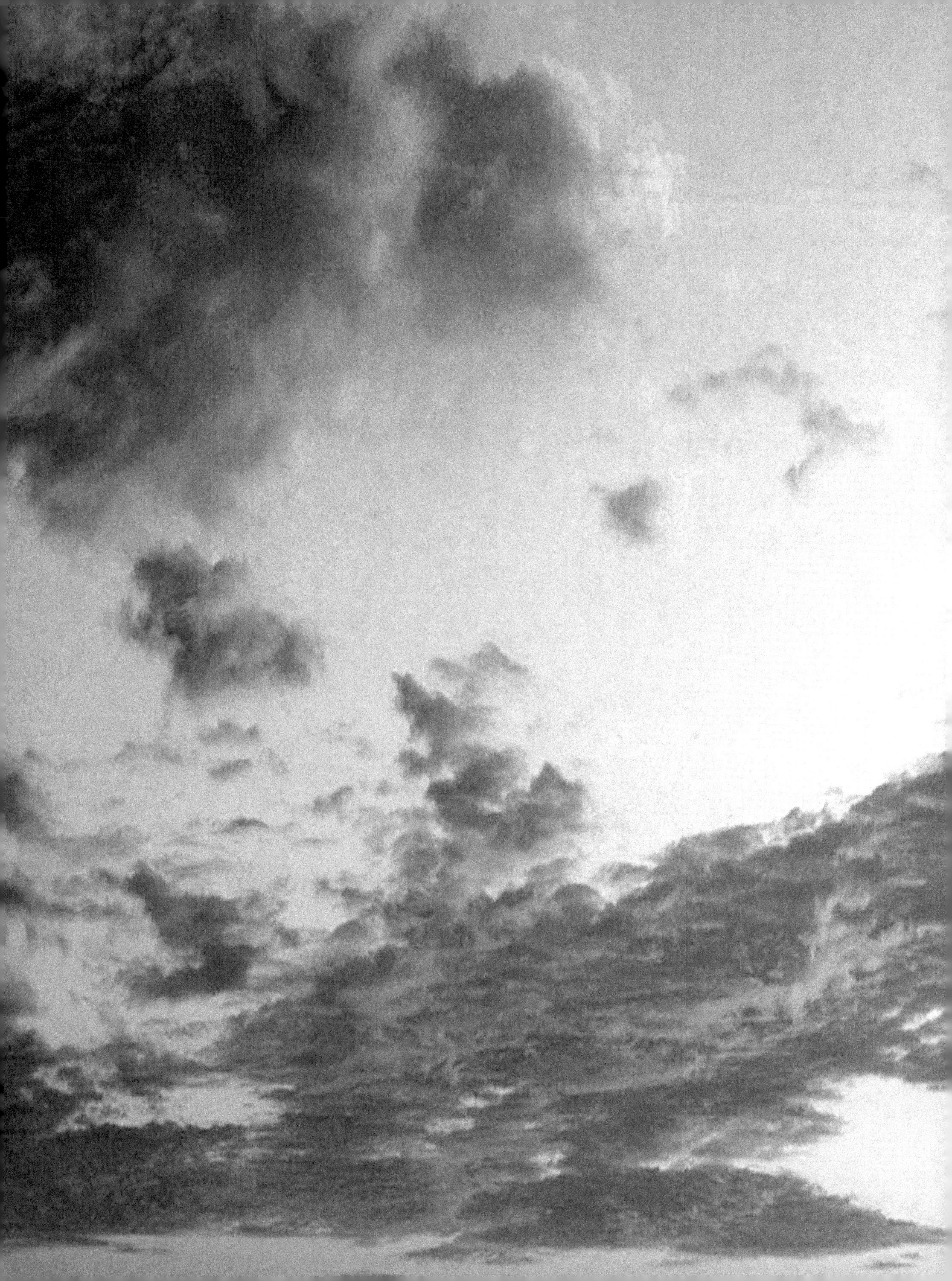

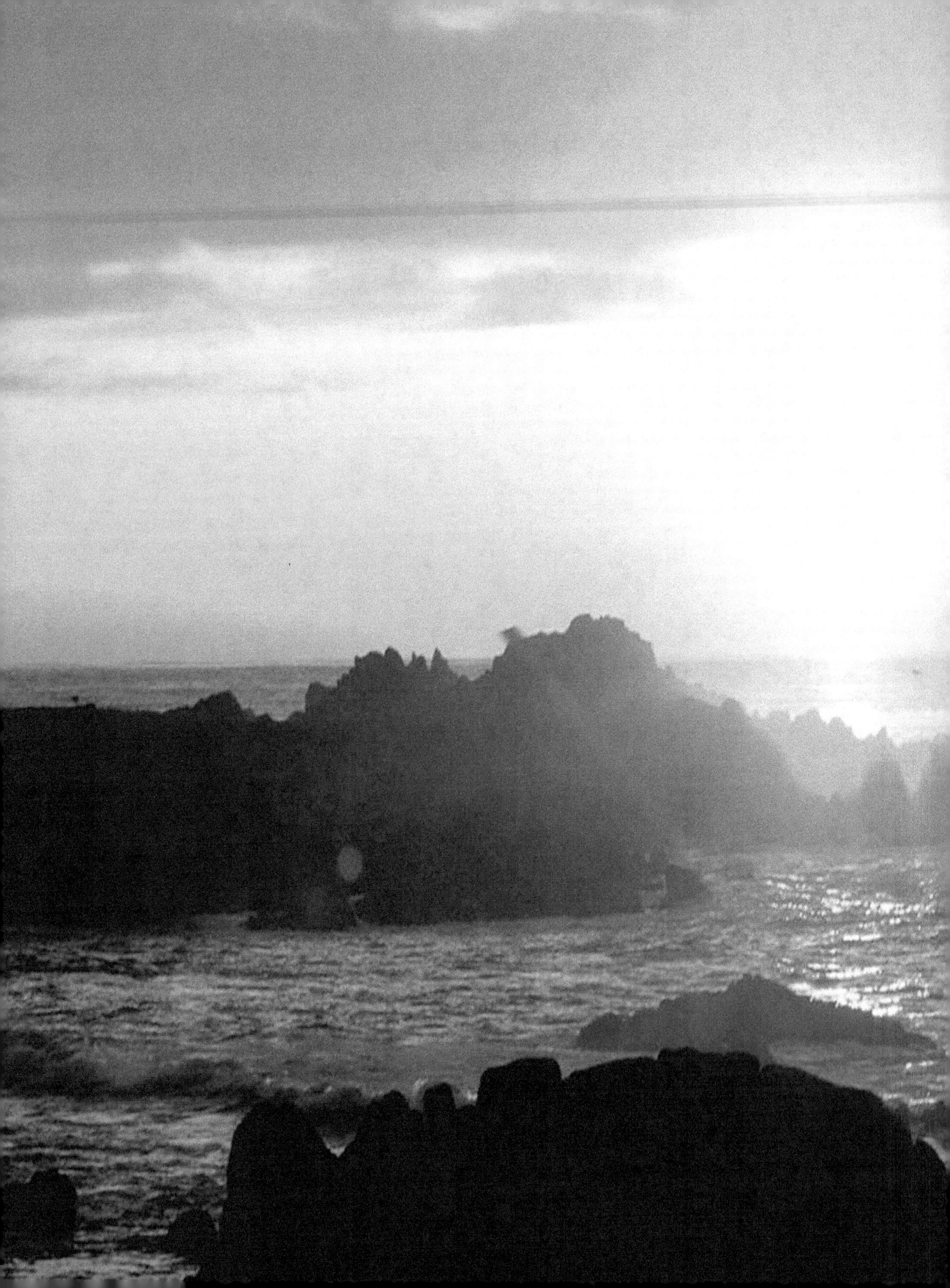

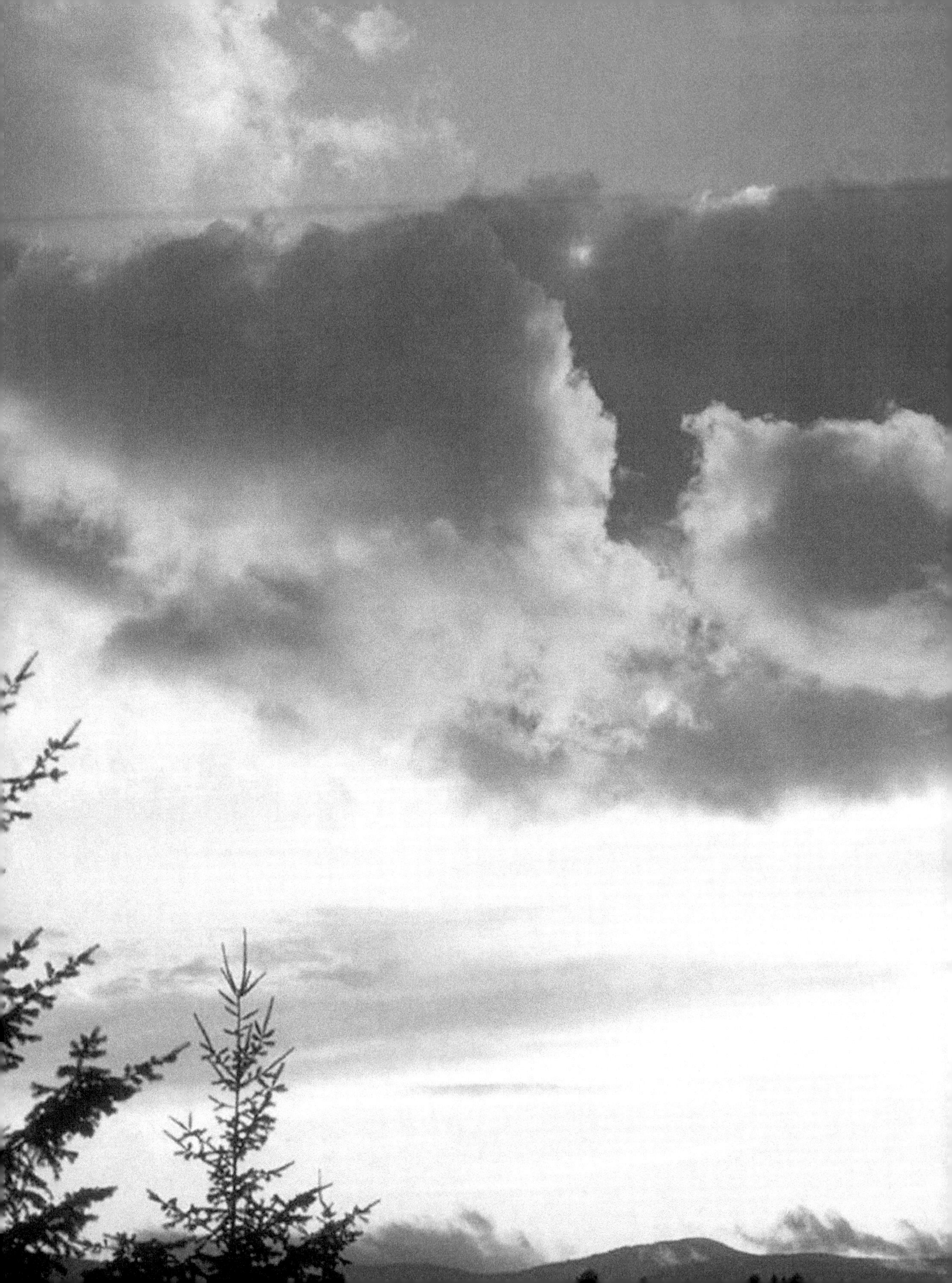

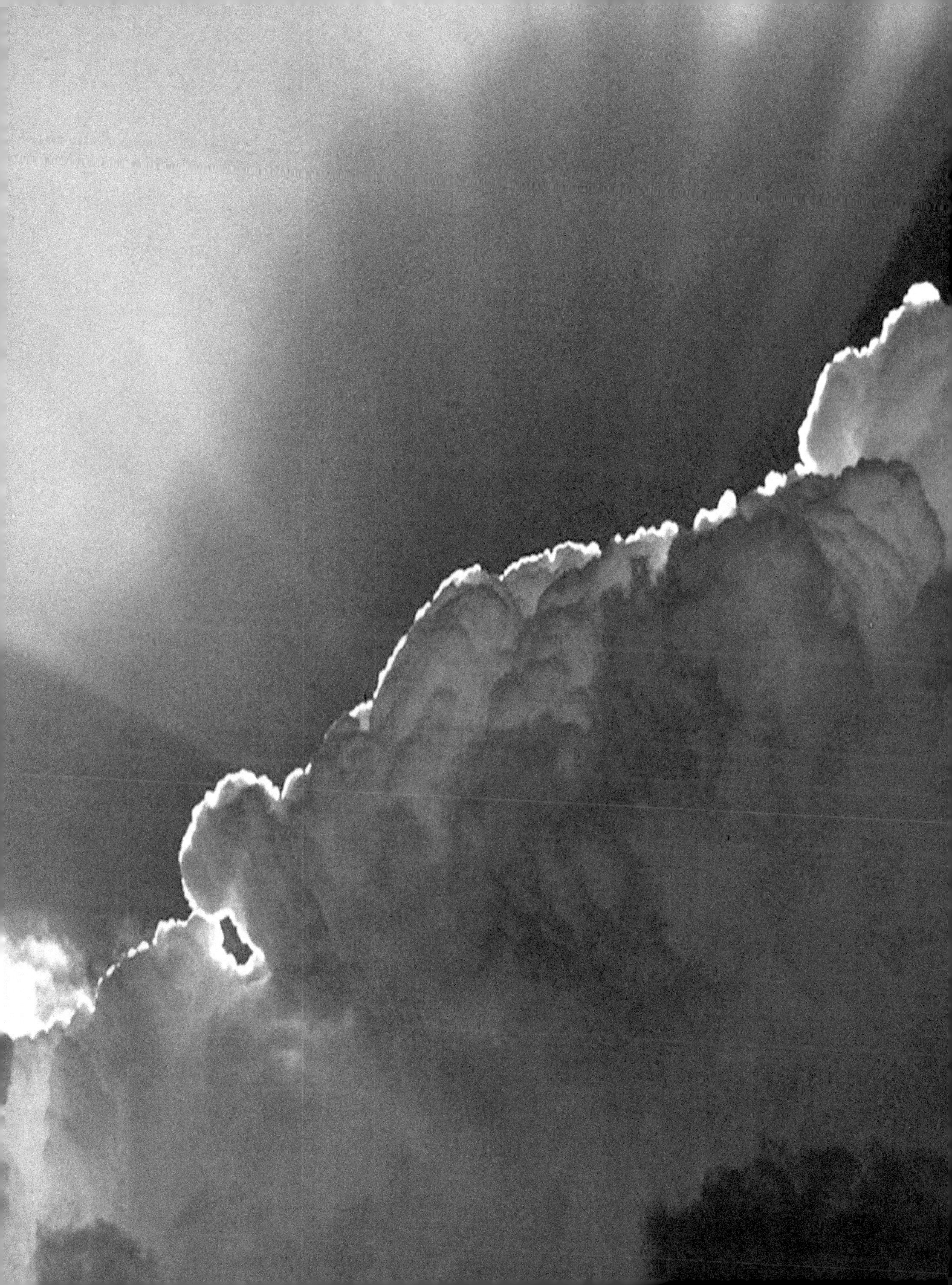

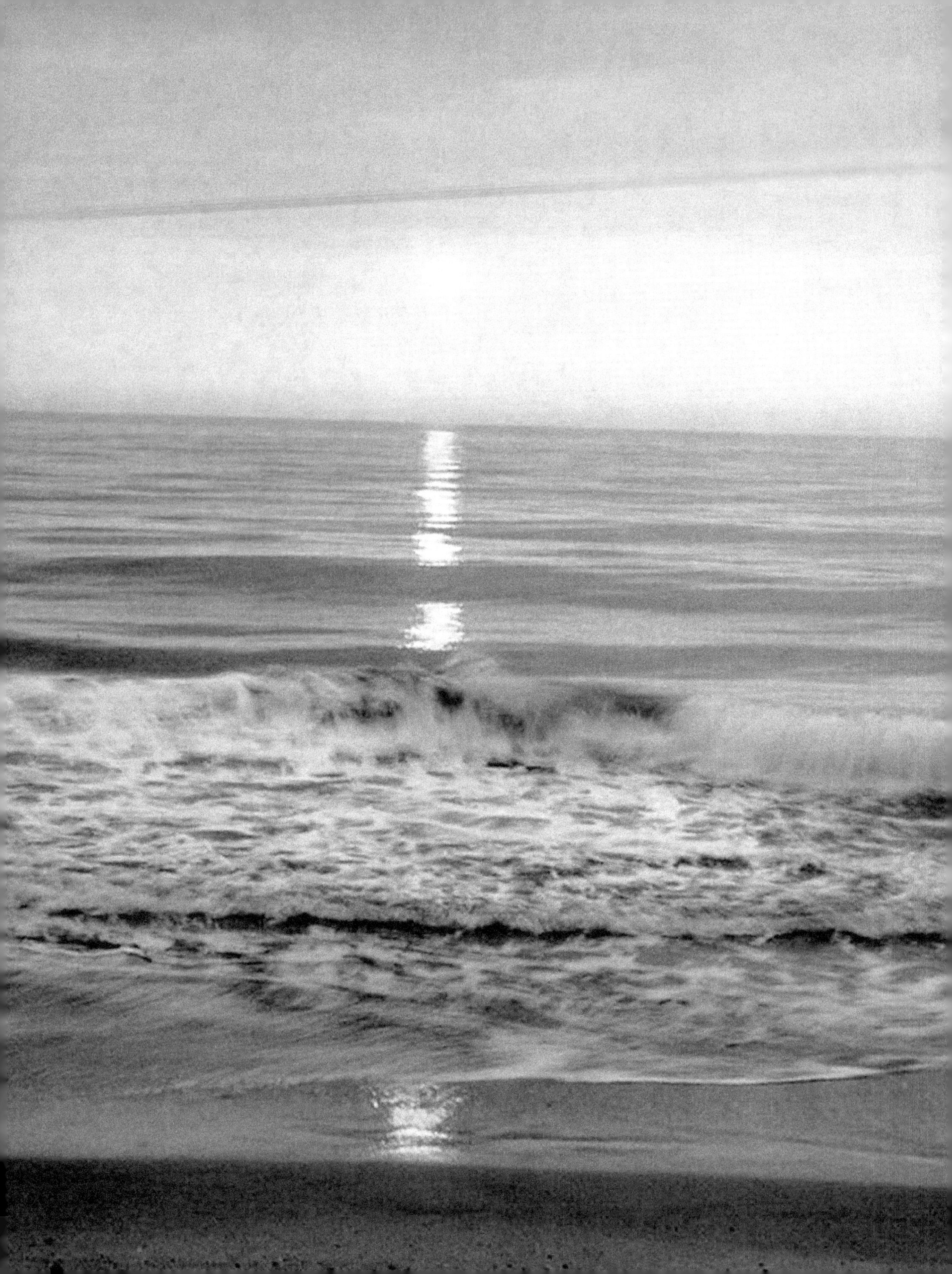

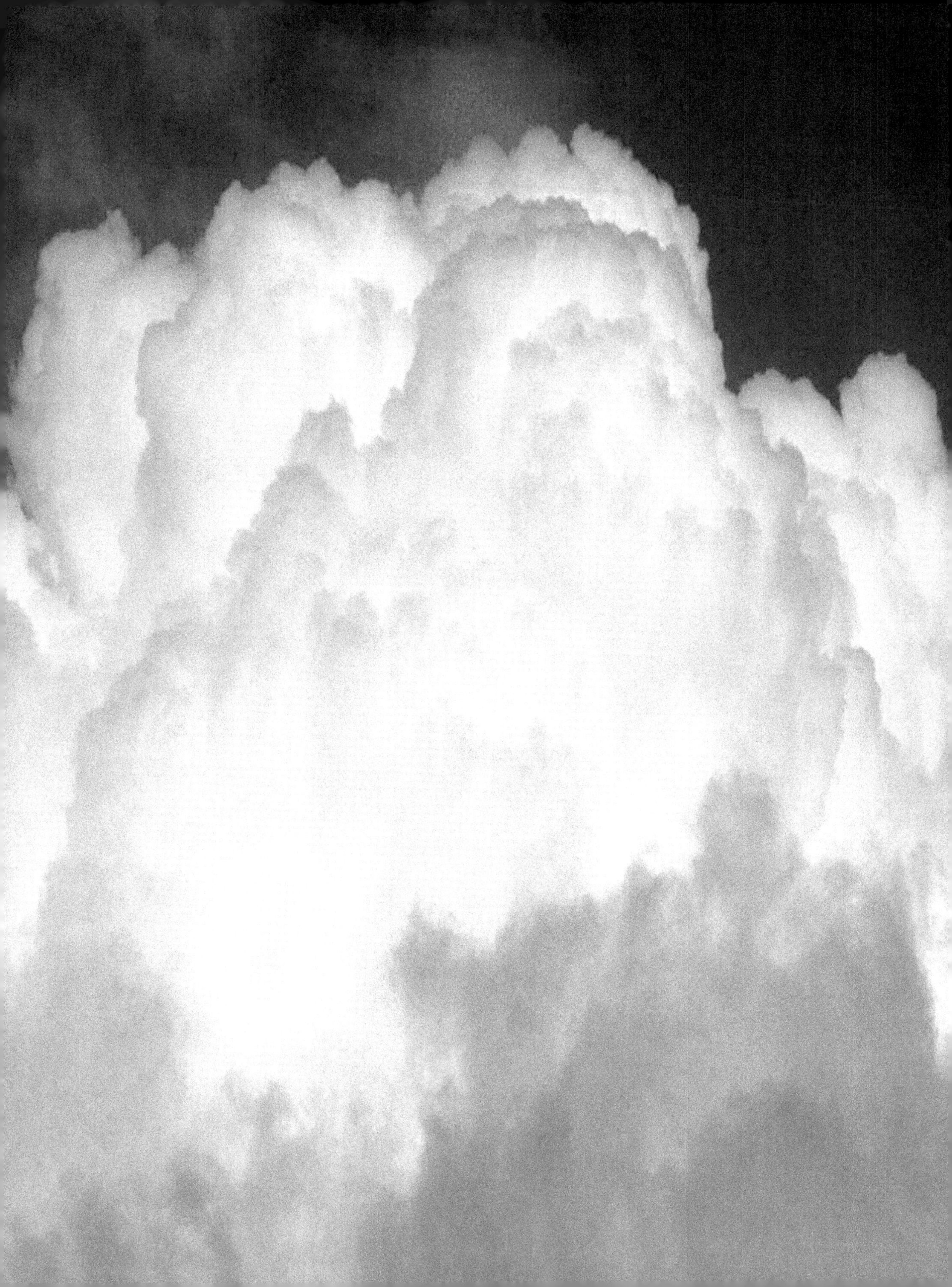

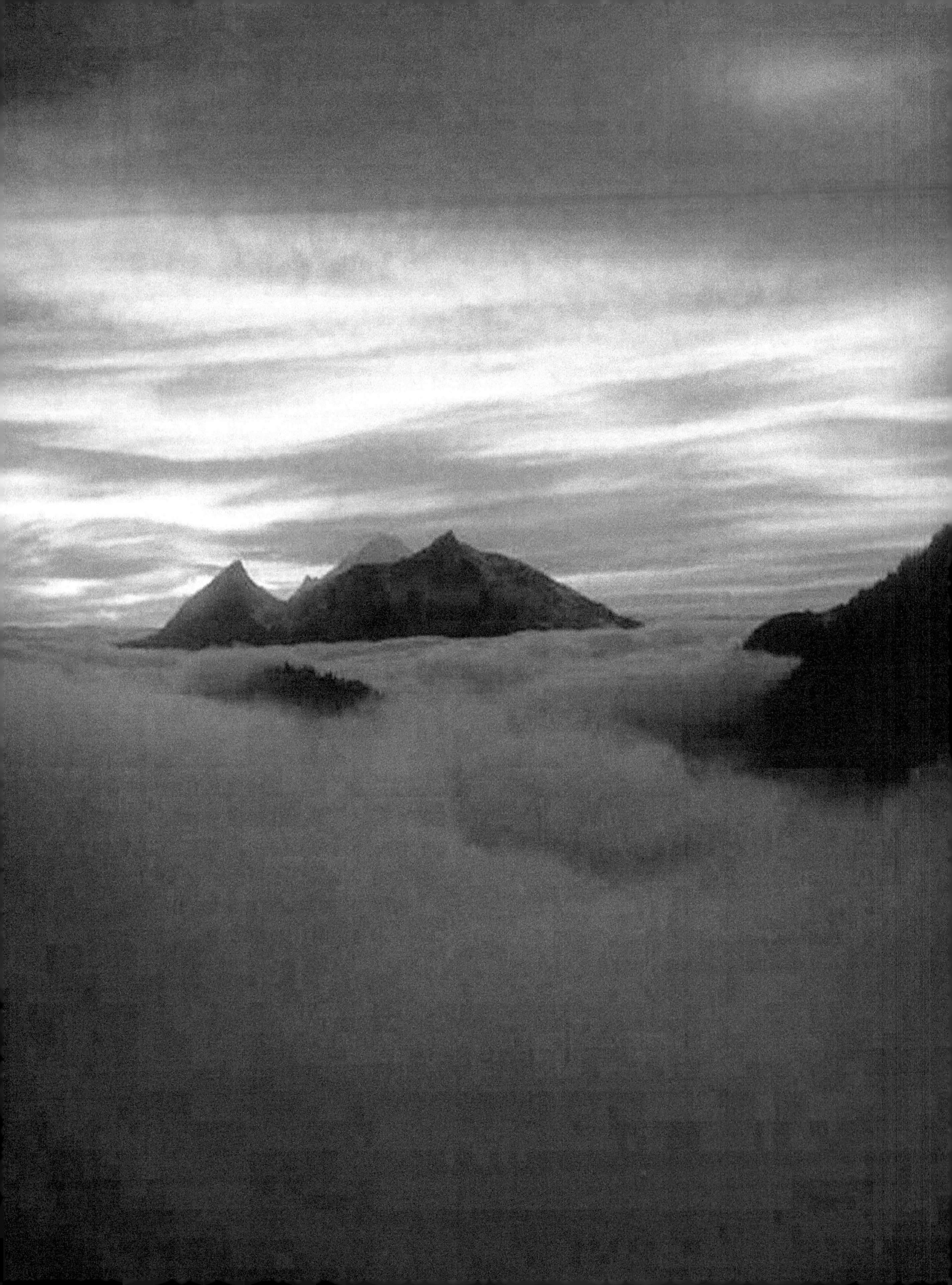

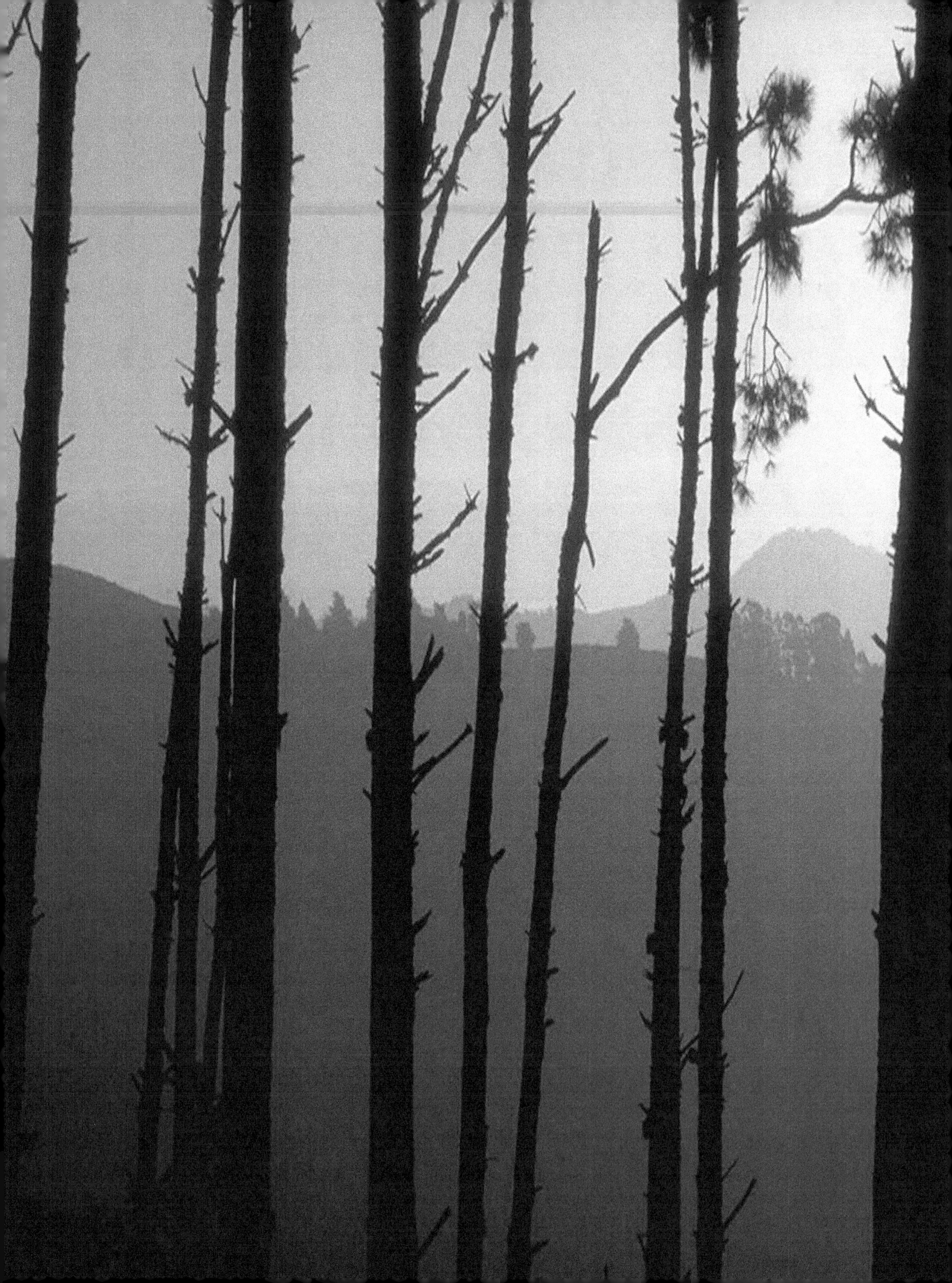

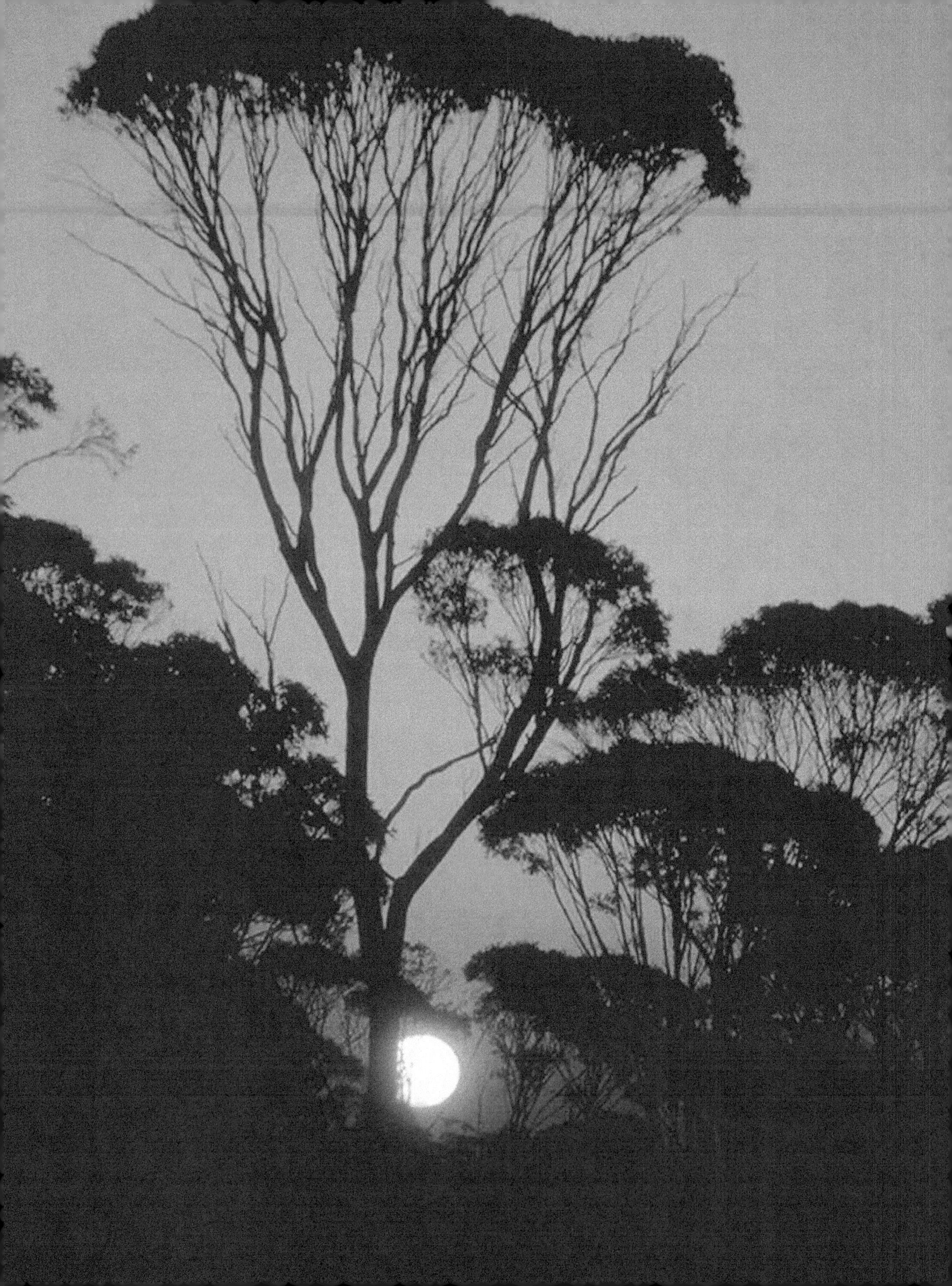

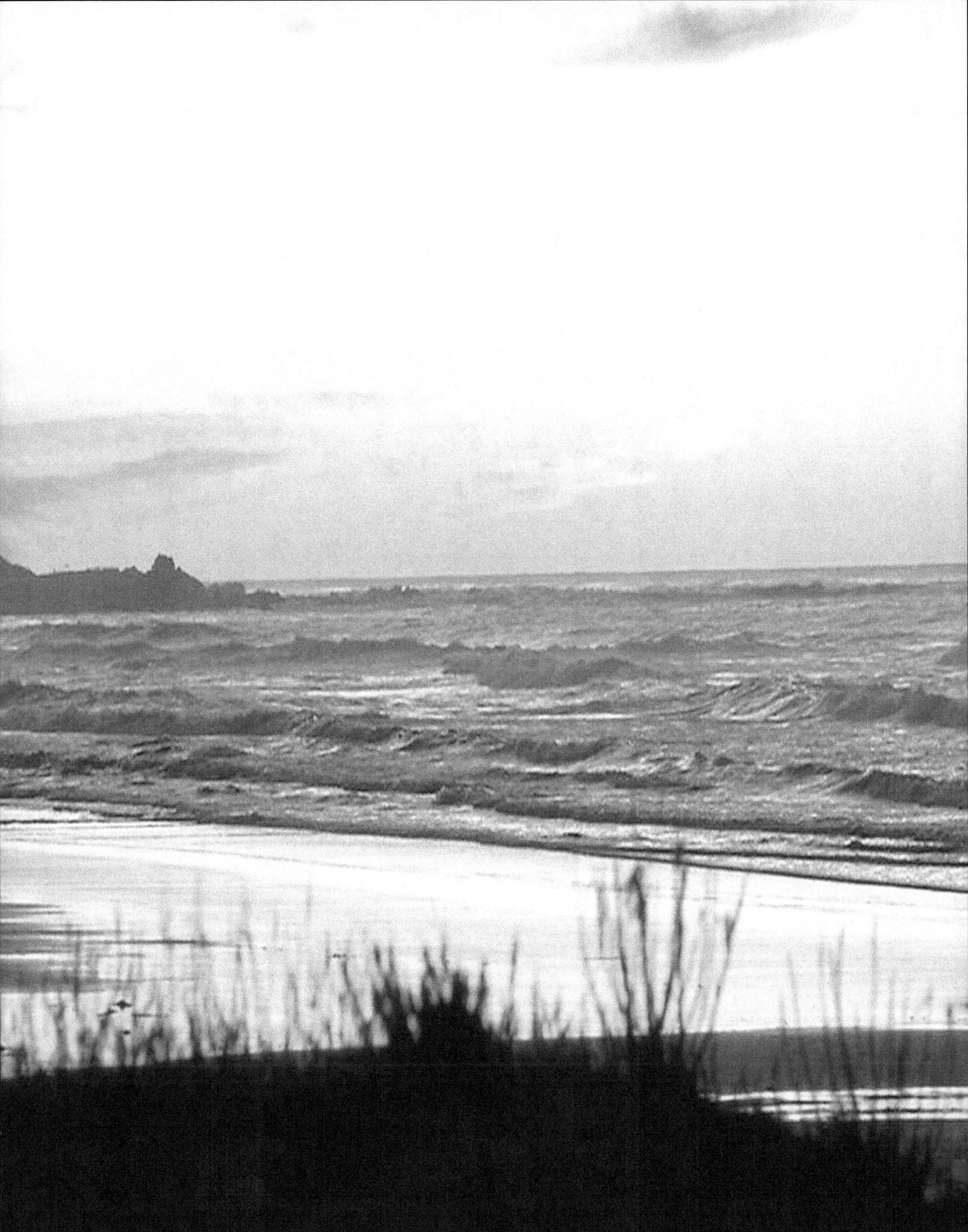

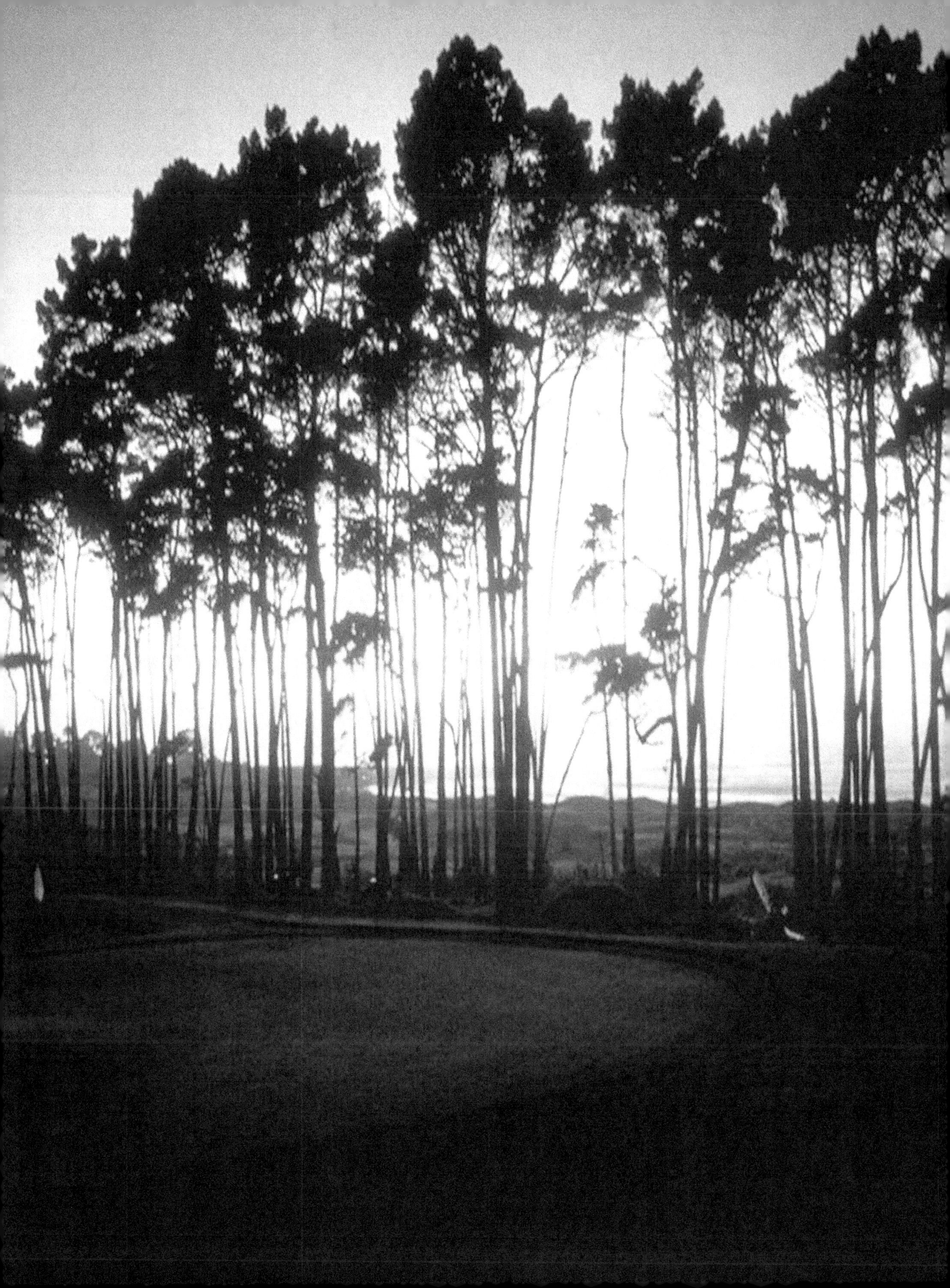

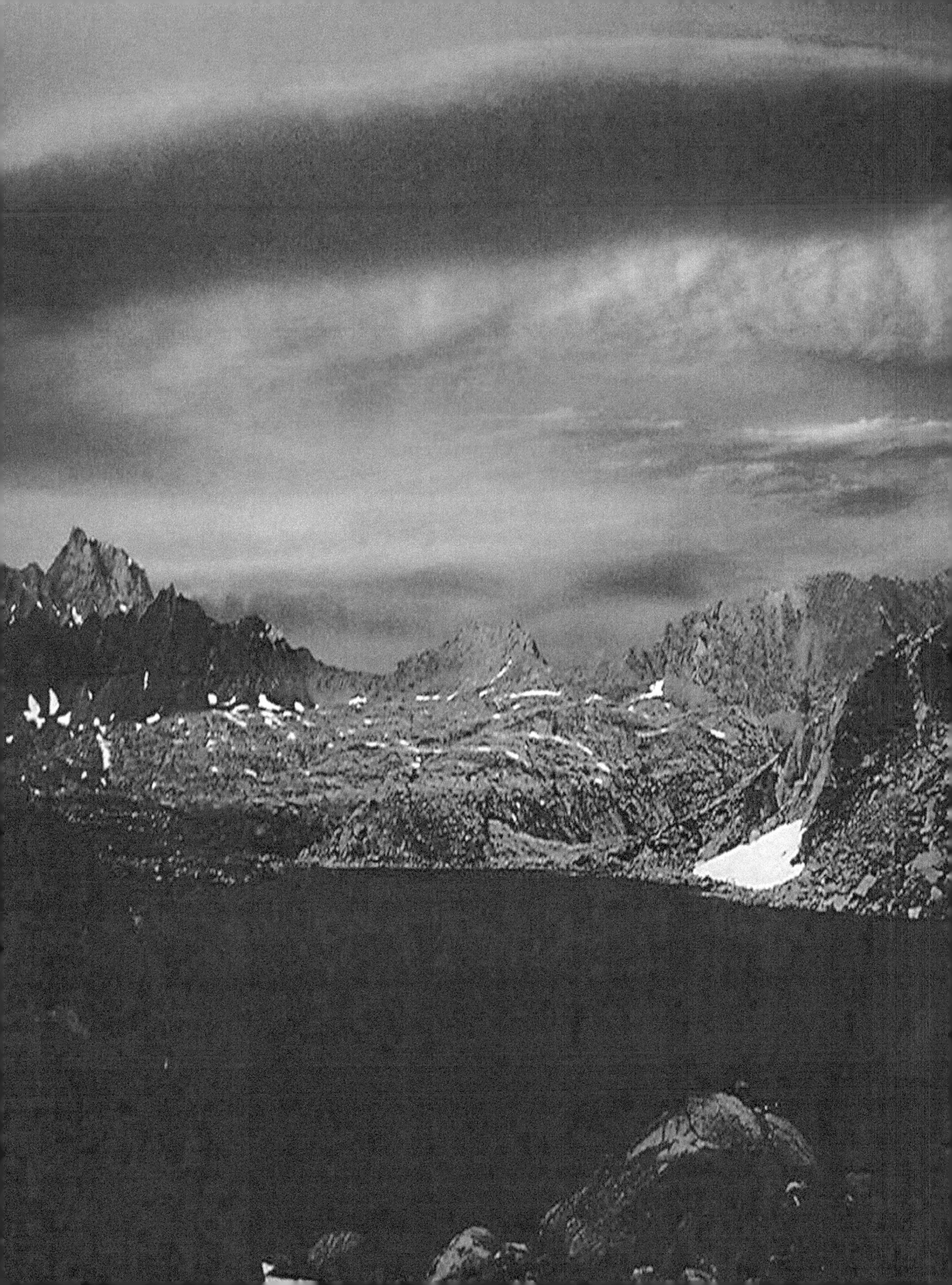

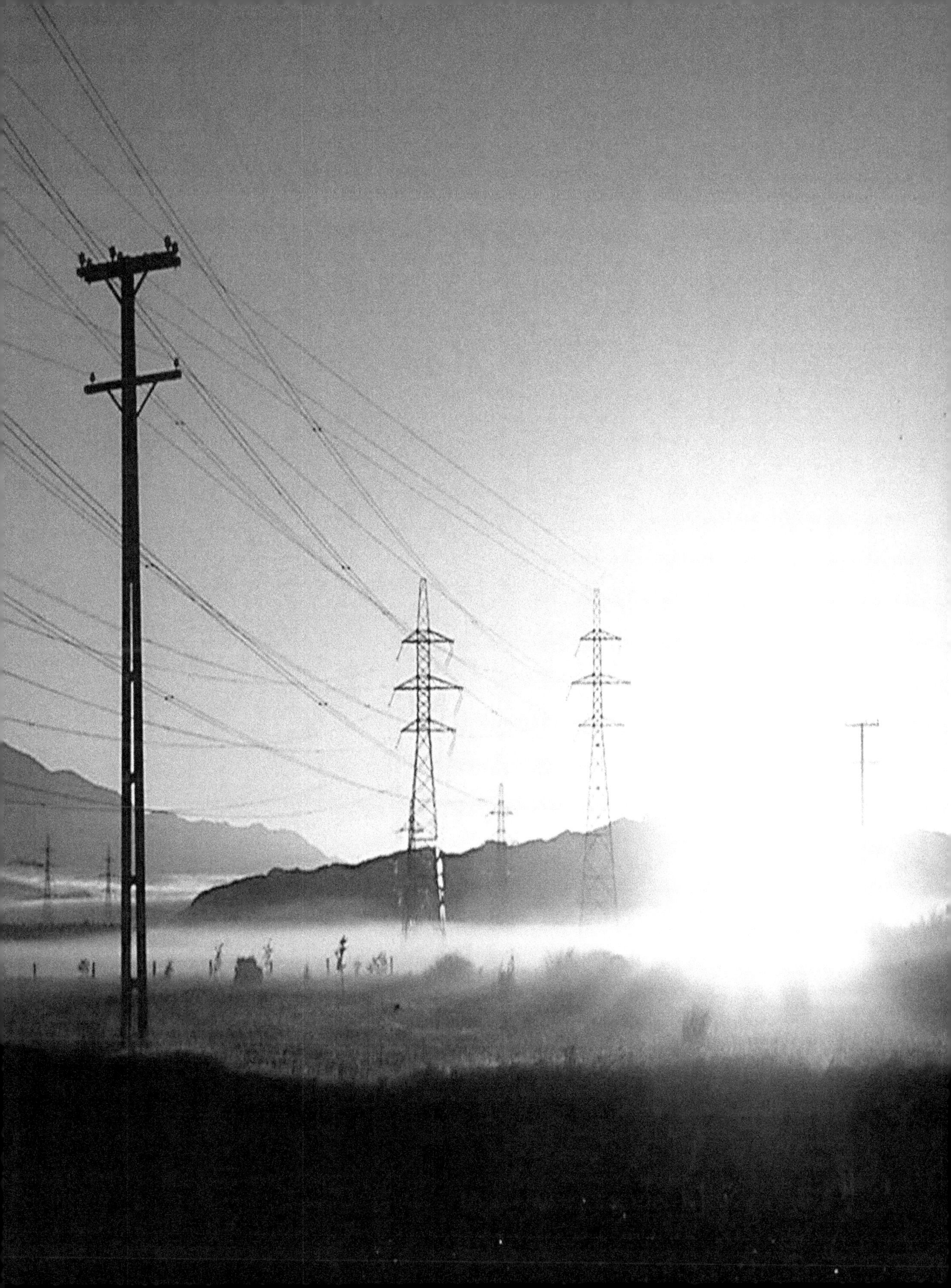

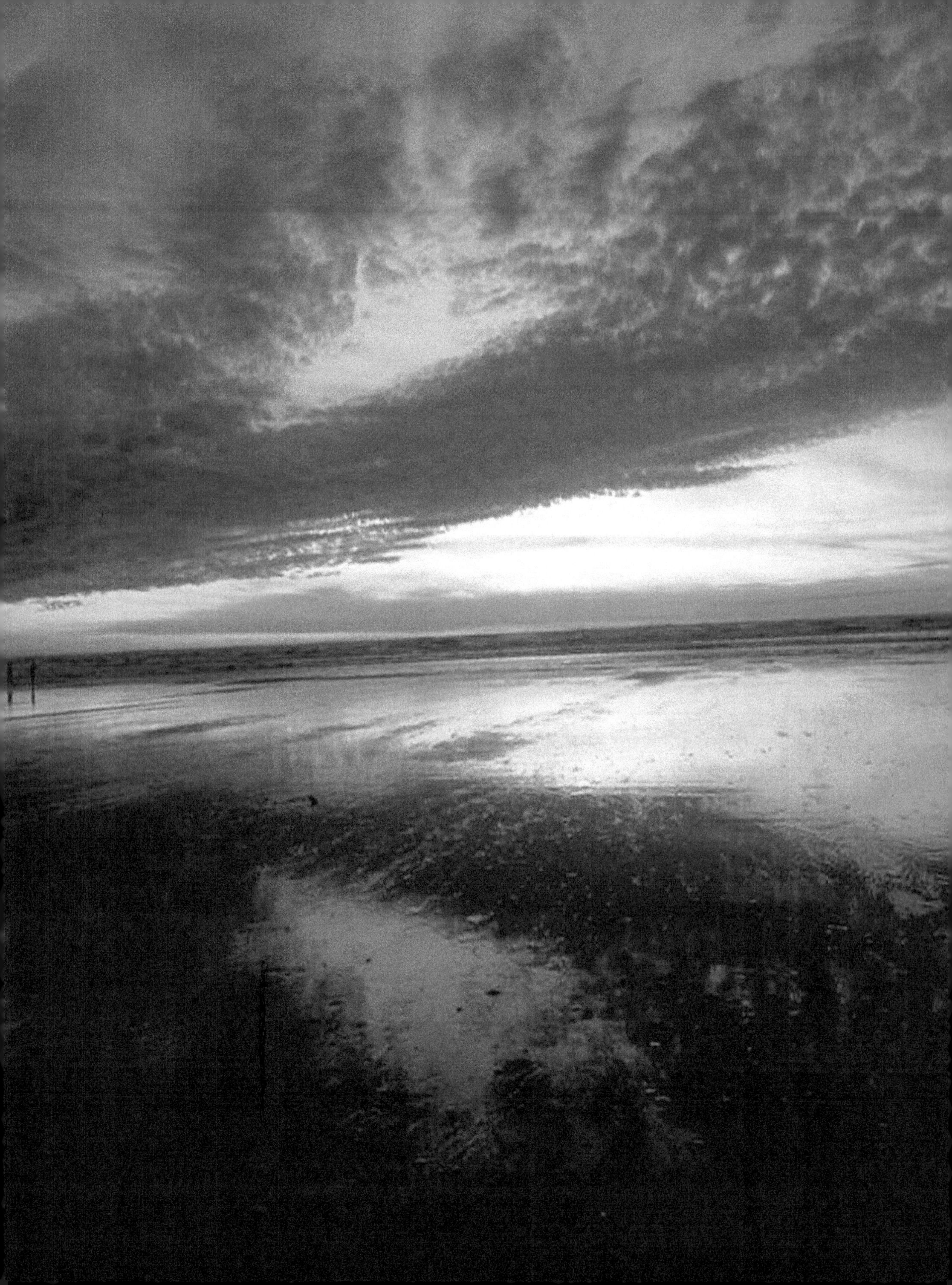

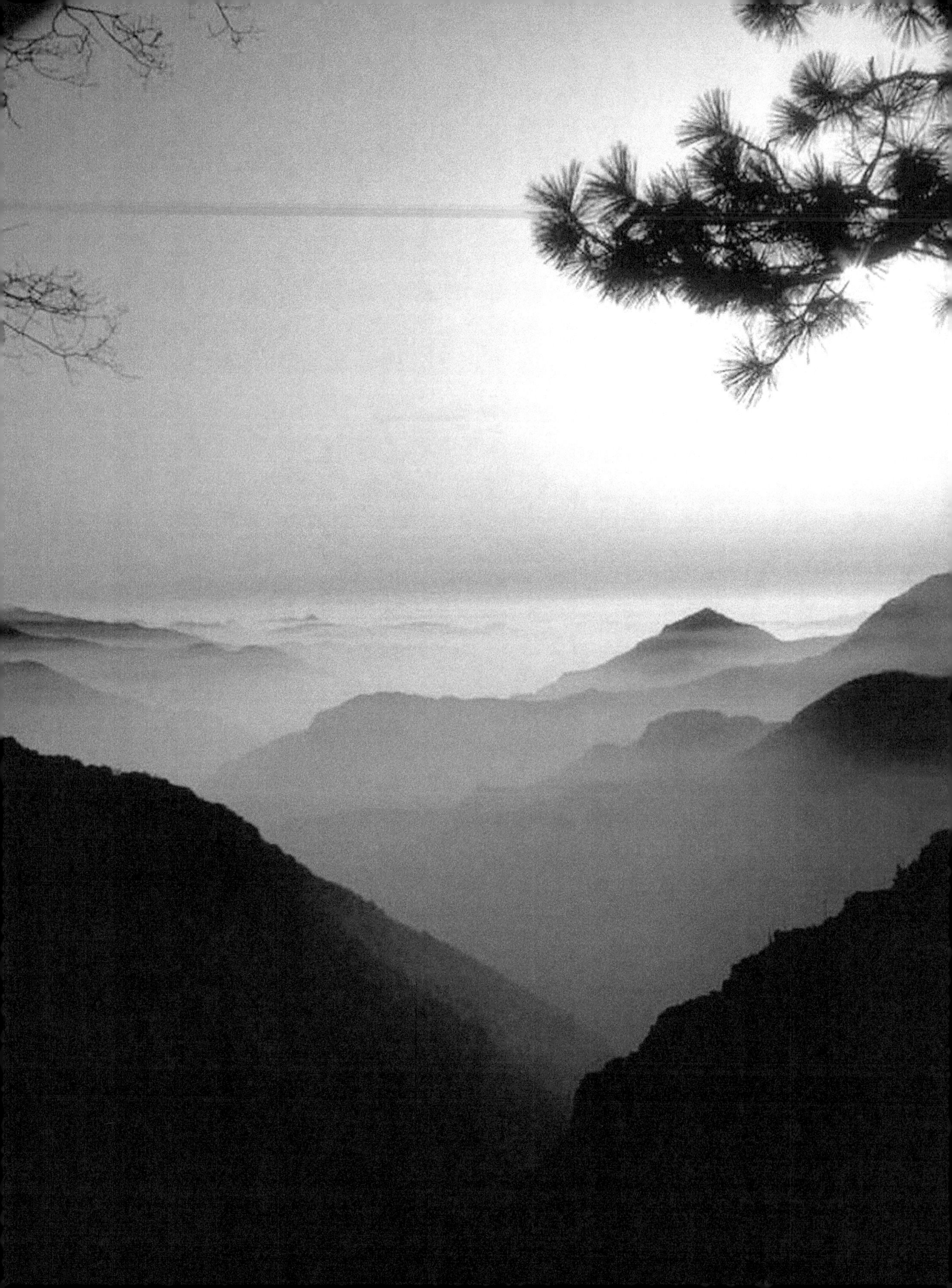

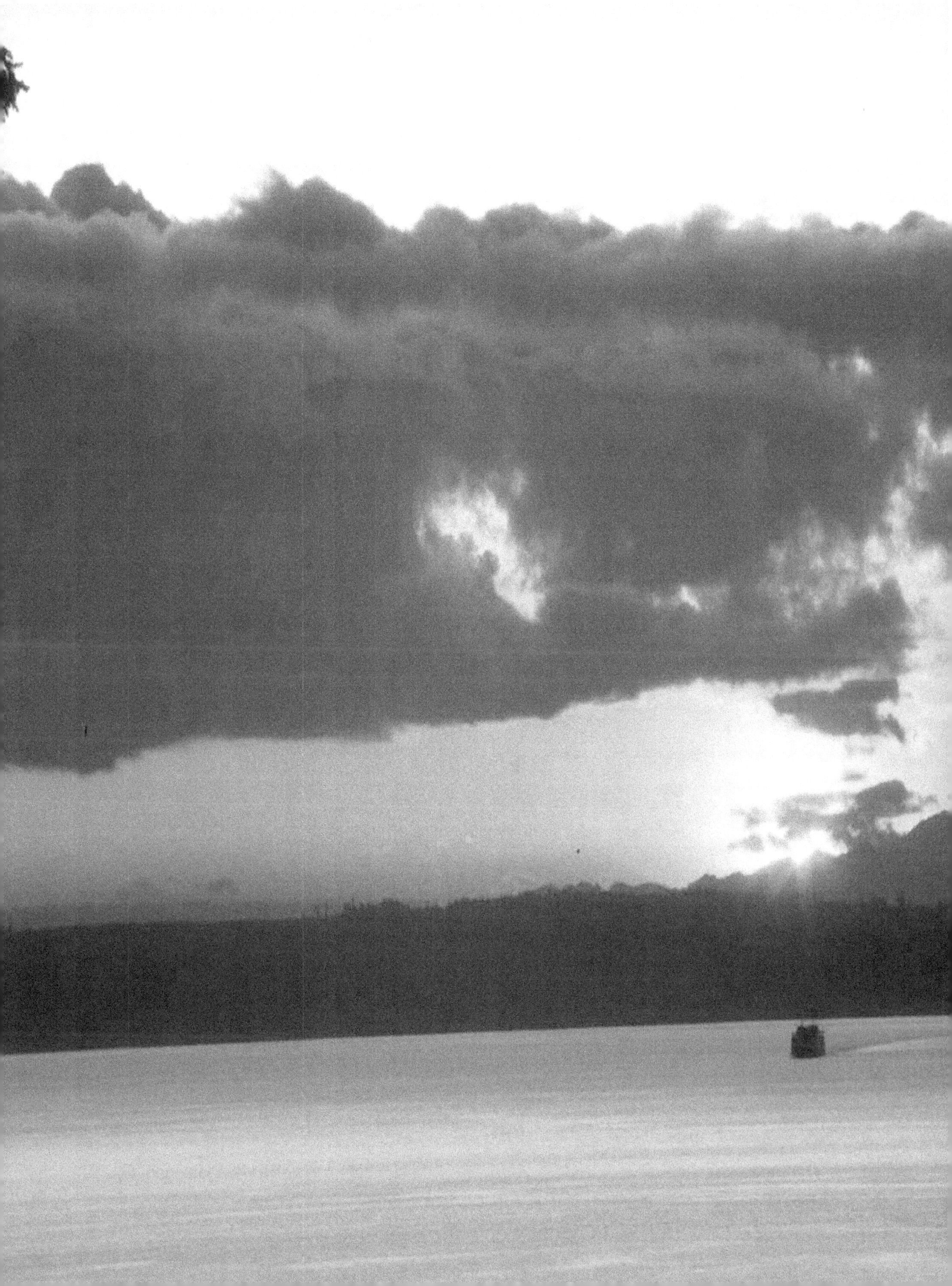

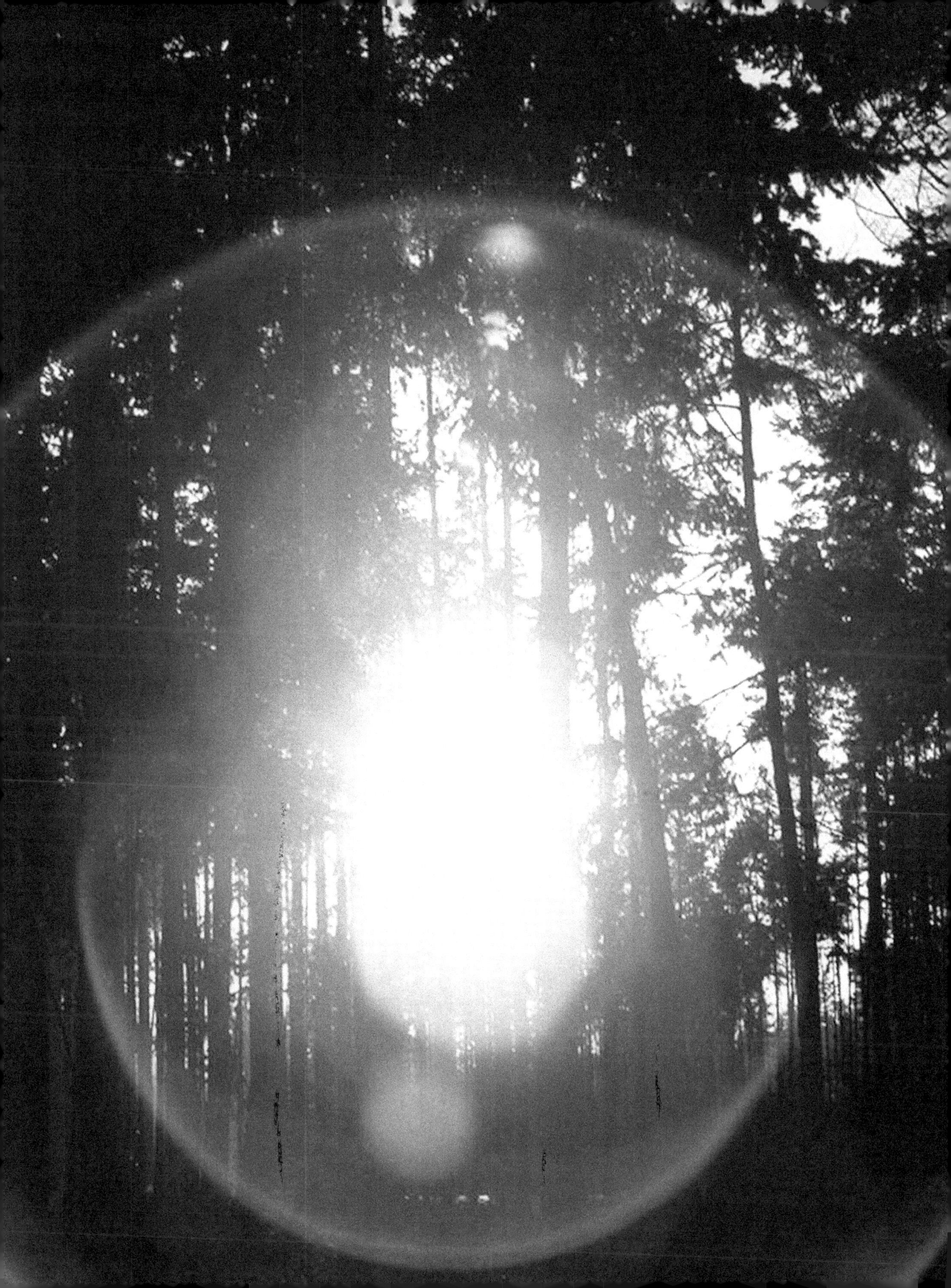

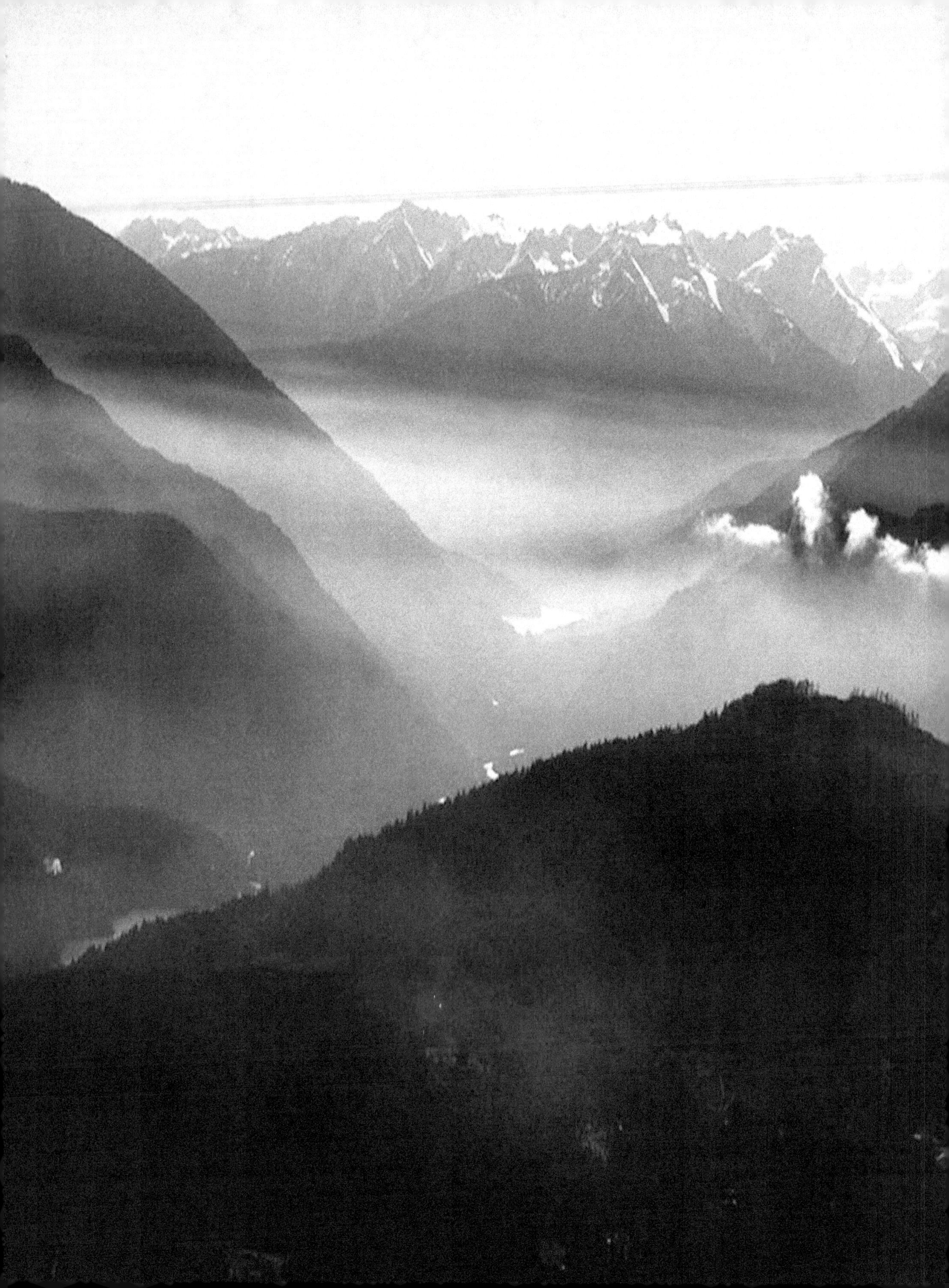

www.ingramcontent.com/pod-product-compliance
Lightning Source LLC
Chambersburg PA
CBHW080600190526
45169CB00007B/2829
9781532875724